LESSONS FROM A VICTIM SUPPORT CRIME PREVENTION PROJECT

Alice Sampson

CRIME PREVENTION UNIT: PAPER NO. 25
LONDON: HOME OFFICE

Editor: Gloria Laycock
Home Office Crime Prevention Unit
50 Queen Anne's Gate
London SW1H 9AT

Crime Prevention Unit Papers

The Home Office Prevention Unit was formed in 1983 to promote preventive action against crime. It has a particular responsibility to disseminate information on crime prevention topics. The object of the present series of occasional papers is to present analysis and research material in a way which should help and inform practitioners whose work can help reduce crime.

ISBN 0 86252 616 7

Foreword

Helping victims of crime and giving crime prevention assistance in inner-city areas is a challenging and difficult task. It is perhaps not suprising, therefore, that the joint victim support/crime prevention initiative described in this report met with mixed results.

The report suggests that successful implementation of a crime prevention project depends upon a number of factors – adequate funding; a minimum project length of perhaps 3 years; a small 'core' inter-agency working group; addressing the fears of the residents as well as the conflicts between them; and helping victims solve practical difficulties and then giving emotional support. Crime problems can be resolved, but this study shows the difficulty of devising answers in areas of mixed race and social and economic deprivation. The purpose of this report is to assist those who plan to rise to these challenges and work together to reduce crime.

I M BURNS
Deputy Under Secretary of State
Home Office
March 1991

Acknowledgements

A great number of people have contributed to this report and to the project. Thanks should first go to the residents on the estate, especially those who gave up their time to be interviewed. The two project workers Natalie Edwardes and Jacqui Hylton made a substantial contribution. So too did the coordinator of victim support Joanna Woodd. It was a pleasure to work with them. Asking Chief Inspector Wright for the incident log data was always 'no problem' – and it wasn't.

Much of the data was analysed by Graham Farrell before he went back to University – a special thanks for all the hard work. Sarah Holdsworth also contributed to some of the data collection. Comments on a draft of the paper from Greta Brooks, Paul Rock and Joanna Woodd were very helpful.

With thanks to everyone.

Alice Sampson
March 1991.

Contents

List of tables

Introduction

Although the problems associated with implementing community crime and fear prevention schemes have been well-documented, the debate on how to overcome these difficulties and achieve tangible results is ongoing (Hope, 1985; Hope and Shaw, 1988; Rosenbaum, 1987, 1988; Skogan, 1988; Lavarakas and Bennett, 1989). The aim of this paper is to contribute to that debate on the basis of experience gained in the course of a two year joint National Association of Victim Support (NAVSS) and Home Office Crime Prevention Unit (CPU) victim support/crime prevention initiative described in CPU paper number 21 (Sampson and Farrell, 1990).

The objectives of the project, set by NAVSS and the CPU, were to support victims of crime and harassment; give them crime prevention advice, and improve the quality of life of residents, through fear reduction activities and by encouraging self help between neighbours. Largely on the basis of a victimisation/crime prevention survey four practical aims were agreed and two part-time project workers were employed to implement these strategies. They were to convene an inter-agency working group, set up care watches, a mothers' and toddlers' group and a community mediation scheme. Later in the project the workers implemented a block watch scheme.

The survey results gave an indication of the extent of victimisation and an impression of life on the estate. A notable proportion of residents suffered from interpersonal violence and threats. Young residents were most at risk and women most vulnerable in or near their homes. Also on the basis of the results, the most under-reported crimes were shown to be domestic and racial attacks and proportionately more burglaries were found in the larger, more run-down blocks of flats. Those most constrained by the fear of crime in public places were usually women who were specifically afraid of being attacked, whilst others who went out at night, but avoided certain places, were generally worried something might happen. There was little formal social interaction between residents; a small minority were members of the tenants' association (TA) and other community groups. At an informal level a third of the respondents had four or more residents as friends and a third had no friends living on the estate. Two-thirds of the respondents watched out for each others flats but this was not found to be effective in reducing burglary.

Within this context, the project workers had to find ways of engendering effective crime prevention activities and encouraging self-referrals and neighbouring. The difficulties encountered by the workers in gaining the trust of residents and assisting them to help themselves, and the lessons learned from these experiences are described in this paper. This is not, however, an investigative paper to apportion 'blame' to a particular agency or person. Rather it is to describe the problems and constructively suggest alternative patterns of working which may have led to a more positive project outcome. The problems, and their possible solutions, are probably typical of other deprived inner-city areas and it is hoped the lessons learned will be applicable to other similar schemes.

The joint project failed to achieve all of its aims but there were some benefits enjoyed by residents as a consequence of the scheme. Victims of crime were supported and some received improved security. Longer term benefits may come about because the victim support/crime prevention initiative raised the profile of the estate with relevant agencies including the local authority. The restructuring of the local housing management and architectural design changes are planned, although, at the time of going to the press, they are still contingent on obtaining central government funding. It is doubtful these plans would have occurred without the crime prevention project on the estate. The knowledge of the workers and the research findings were used extensively to make recommendations for changes.

The research for this project has a number of limitations. From an early stage it became evident that the process of implementation was an important part of the evaluation and the researcher's role evolved into action research (in other words, research findings were regularly fedback to the workers, and when appropriate, they changed their working practices accordingly). Many of the findings in this report therefore come from conversations with the workers, tenants' association representatives, notes and observations of meetings and from interviews with victims and members of the working group. Although the numbers of people interviewed are small, many of the conversations were in-depth and took place over a two year period. The consistency of the views and actions taken by these people enable some general conclusions to be drawn from the findings. The length of the report however only allows for a brief discussion of some of the lessons learned.

Originally it was proposed to have a "before", and "after" victimisation survey and compare the results to assess its success. A second victimisation survey was not undertaken by the CPU on the grounds that the ongoing crime prevention activities were too limited to justify the expense. As a consequence it is not possible to make any statements about residents who have not been a victim of a reported crime (or visited the project office) within the last two years or to make any statements about their fear. Another shortcoming is that a wide range of issues and topics relevant to assessing the project arose during the two years and there was not enough time to give each problem sufficient in-depth consideration to recommend a possible solution with any certainty. In particular more work was needed on the training of the project workers, 'problem' families, multi-victims, neighbour disputes and safety strategies undertaken by residents as part of their everyday lives.

The following seven sections discuss the problems encountered in implementing each aim and some lessons learned are drawn from each. Concluding comments place the project in a broader context of implementation difficulties experienced by local crime prevention initiatives.

The Planning Phase

With the benefit of hindsight shortcomings at the planning phase contributed to the difficulties encountered at the implementation stage. The most significant elements in this phase are outlined below. Suggestions are also made on possible improvements which may have facilitated the subsequent implementation process.

(i)   Management Structure

The project was set up with two sources of funding, the project workers salary paid by the NAVSS and the research by the CPU. It was acknowledged from the outset that the main objectives of the two funding bodies were different in emphasis, NAVSS being concerned to improve service delivery to victims of crime in high crime areas of the inner city and CPU concerned to reduce crime. It was assumed these priorities were complimentary and in practice would need to be dealt with together. In the event, the difference in focus between the two funding bodies resulted in some difficulties during the implementation phase.

A management structure for the project was not finalised until February 1989, eight months after the project had begun. This, and the conflicts involved in sorting out the structure, caused uncertainty for the project workers, from which they never recovered. Both NAVSS and CPU retained a managerial input into the project and this had the effect of separating the crime prevention tasks from the victim support work. The workers often talked of "our work for the Home Office" meaning crime prevention work, and "our work for the National" referring to giving emotional support and immediate practical assistance to victims. Both the workers and the victim support coordinator felt as if they were being pulled in different directions by NAVSS and the CPU and this lowered their morale and enthusiasm for the project. There were times when the work was extremely difficult and the workers and the coordinator felt they received little positive support and were blamed for the problems they encountered.

(ii)   Groundwork

Early on it became apparent that insufficient thought and attention had been given to the initial groundwork. The first estate chosen became the site of another project and a local councillor suggested an alternative estate because there was no community infrastructure. Community workers knew this estate was difficult to work on and previous attempts to get youth groups, old age pensioners clubs and mothers' and toddlers' groups off the ground had all been short-lived. Support for the project from the residents was far from unanimous; some were sceptical about Home Office involvement; some felt better housing management was most important, others thought a crime prevention project would be better off on another near-by estate where their problems were worse, whilst others thought a crime prevention project would give the estate a bad reputation it did not deserve. At a general TA meeting a vote was taken against letting the project workers u e the TA flat as an office and empty shop premises were found instead.

Tensions between the tenants' association representatives and the project workers fluctuated throughout the two years, and whilst this may to some extent be a

3

feature of projects which are initiated by 'outsiders' rather than being grassroots in conception, there are a number of ways in which they can be minimised. It is better to choose an estate (or area) where the crime and crime-related problems are perceived by the residents to be bad *and* to be getting worse; where there is a tenants' association capable of working together to tackle the problems in their area; and where an identifiable group of residents are willing to participate in a project.

Thus, time spent choosing an appropriate area, canvassing the views of the residents and workers and statutory and voluntary agencies, is time well spent. Once a location has been chosen the groundwork in preparation for the introduction of a project is equally important. For this initiative the results of a victimisation survey provided the information baseline but there were a number of problems with these data. The most useful information was about each block but since there was a survey response rate of 62% and this rate varied across blocks, a very small number of residents responded from some blocks of flats. This made it difficult to draw reliable conclusions on an individual block basis. The second problem was that, even though the questionnaire was piloted, some key problems were not picked up in the survey results, for example, the dynamics of the residents' social life (particularly the divisiveness between some residents), the problem of vandalism by young children, and the impact of a few 'problem' families.

A more suitable approach may have been for the workers and researcher to have interviewed residents from a representative sample of the different sizes of blocks of flats using semi-structured interview schedules. This would have started a consultation process with many residents at an early stage and would have been a useful way to generate enthusiasm for the project and pave the way for a successful initiative (see, for example, Safe Neighbourhood Unit, 1985). This approach also enables the workers to develop a working knowledge of life on the estate and get to know some residents before taking on referrals. With a company undertaking a survey it took nearly a year for the workers to develop this knowledge.

(iii) Selection of staff

The job description for the workers specified a community development approach to achieving the prevention of crime. Most of the applicants were under 30 years of age with some experience of working in areas of caring and advisory work. No workers from other agencies associated with the criminal justice system applied to be seconded to the project, a characteristic of some other initiatives (Forrester et al., 1988). The work required a high degree of commitment and the hours of work were un-social.

It is not clear whether the secondment of workers from other agencies is better than the employment of workers without previous experience in the criminal justice system, for implementing an effective crime prevention project (or that this is a necessary distinction to make). There were, however, three factors to which the workers' reactions and coping mechanisms seemed to be important.

4

First, is their probable reactions to the neighbourhood aura. Where residents are despondent, fragmented and 'don't want to know' it seems that established grassroots workers, be it the police, social workers, community workers or probation officers, absorb these feelings and they become part of their work attitude. Similarly workers employed to implement a scheme can, and do, adopt these negative feelings about the area and the residents. It is difficult to effectively implement an initiative unless the workers are able to break this cycle of despondency and identify some alternative and positive ways of working.

Secondly, is a worker's ability to understand both the formal and informal political complexities of the locality. At one level, there are the central/local government relations and relations between different statutory and voluntary agencies, and at another, the importance of social relations between residents and between residents and grassroots workers from those agencies.

Thirdly, working in deprived high-crime areas with victims of crime is stressful. Workers who live in similar environments are continually subjected to such stress. Both workers were themselves victims several times during the two years and one of the workers described herself as "one of society's victims". Yet these workers are probably better able to understand the plight of victims. Whatever type of worker is selected, an active routinised support system would seem to be necessary.

The workers were undoubtedly important but the extent of this influence is difficult to assess. One of the neglected areas of this report is for example, an analysis of appropriate staff training. A training programme sensitive to the needs of the implementation strategies would probably have had a positive effect. One area which the workers found particularly difficult was in giving crime prevention advice. They had no previous experience and they received little crime prevention training.

(iv) Access to resources

In the first year of the project no attempt was made by the workers or the coordinator of victim support to raise funds for the project. Once it became apparent that security improvements were often too costly for residents, funds were obtained from the Home Office and from trusts of local companies. Funding was also obtained to extend the project beyond its experimental two years. Victim support arranged for National Association for Care and Resettlement of Offenders (NACRO) to give burglary prevention advice and fit security hardware free of charge and organised for a portacabin to be given to the scheme.

Improving security in run-down areas is bound to be expensive since some of the improvements necessarily involve replacing rotten windows and weak door frames. The research findings suggested that a reduction of fear would stem from better communal security and this proved to be very expensive to install. The necessity of funds and the ability of the organisers of a project to raise large sums of money seems to be a prerequisite for any crime reduction programme.

(v) Time scale

It is doubtful whether two years is enough time for any community crime prevention project to have an impact in an area without a community infrastructure, where there is a high rate of interpersonal violence, the housing stock is run-down and there are numerous 'signs of crime'. There are no short cuts to gaining the trust of residents and encouraging self-referrals. Fund raising is another time consuming task and trusts often pay out money a few times each year. A well-planned project can reduce the time workers take to be accepted by the residents, and early successes probably ensure the project will have more impact sooner, but three years is likely to be a minimum time.

(vi) Exit strategy

The working group spent most of its meetings in the last six months discussing the future of the project. With hindsight, it would have been a better policy to have thought about this at the beginning and at least mapped out the possible broad options for ending the funded phase of the project. Unless some activities are designed to continue beyond the funding period the residents feel they have been 'experimented' on and this leaves them disillusioned, cynical and more resistant to outsiders and other opportunities to reduce crime.

Victim referrals and crime prevention advice

One of the purposes of the project was for the workers to visit every victim of reported or unreported crime and harassment. This was based on the belief that the more victims the workers supported and gave crime prevention advice to, the more crime and the fear of crime would be reduced and residents would enjoy a better quality of life. To achieve this the workers needed to have personal contact with as many victims as possible. It was hoped that a large proportion of their work would come from self-referrals.

Details on the victims of recorded crime came from the police and are summarised in Table 1. 34% of these crimes were against the person which compared to a national average of 6% (Home Office, 1989) and indicates a high level of violence.

Table 1 (see note 4) shows that 46 households or residents were victims of more than one reported crime. These victims accounted for 38% (111) of the crimes. 20 of the households suffered from property and personal crimes (2 of these were multi-burglary victims and are therefore counted twice); 20 from at least two property crimes (13 from burglary and another property crime, for example, theft or criminal damage, and 7 from burglaries only); and 8 people were repeat victims of interpersonal crimes only. Of these 46 multiple victims; in 10 cases it is not known if the incidents were related or unrelated; in 23 cases, the workers thought they were unrelated; and in 13 cases the incidents were related (they were either domestic attacks, neighbour disputes or the offender was known but did not live in the same flat or next door).

Table 1

Police referrals to the project

Recorded Crime	Number of referrals		
	First Year	Second Year	Total
Burglary	39	27	66
Attempted burglary	8	4	12
Burglary artifice	12	3	15
Theft from households	9	2	11
Other theft (e.g. bicycles)	6	5	11
Theft from motor vehicles	5	8	13
Theft of motor vehicles	8	2	10
Criminal damage	19	18	37
Arson	6	3	9
Rape/attempted rape	3	1	4
Sexual assault	1	—	1
Indecent exposure	1	3	4
Wounding	10	4	14
Assault	24	15	39
Threats	—	2	2
Robbery	14	9	23
Theft person	6	6	12
Other (non crime)	6	—	6
TOTAL	177	112	289

Notes:
1.   The first year was from August 1988 to the end of July 1989 and the second year was from August 1989 to July 1990.
2.   All the crimes recorded by the police were referred to the project.
3.   18 of the assaults and 2 criminal damage incidents were domestic violence.
4.   30 households or householders were referred twice; 13 three times and 3 four times.

Of the referrals in table 1 all the victims received a letter asking them to contact the workers if they wanted any help. 45% were visited and 5% were telephoned. Few residents came to the office in response to the letter (17) and approximately 10 victims were uncooperative at the doorstep when the workers visited them (but no-one actually slammed the door in their face).

It was eight months before self-reported referrals occured. All the self-referrals in the first year had no previous contact with the workers. In the second year self-referred crimes nearly doubled (see table 2). 21 (42%) of all the self-reported crimes were also reported to the police.

7

Table 2

Crimes reported to the project workers by victims

Crime	First Year	Second Year	Total
	Number of Allegations		
Burglary (including attempts)	2	11	13
Burglary artifice	1	2	3
Criminal damage	1	6	7
Arson	1	2	3
Wounding	1	2·	3
Assault	2	2	4
Robbery	—	1	1
Theft person	2	—	2
Domestic attacks	3	2	5
Threats	4	3	7
Sexual assault	1	—	1
Indecent assault	1	—	1
TOTAL	19	31	50

Since it was expected that unreported crime would account for three quarters of all the crime on the estate and the majority of these would be domestic and racial attacks (see CPU paper 21) table 2 would suggest that relatively few unreported crimes were brought to the attention of the workers. One incident of racial abuse was self-reported (an assault), and only five domestic disputes.

Part of the service to victims by workers was to give crime prevention advice. There were records of advice given, or not given, to 154 households or householders. Table 3 summarises this information by type of crime.

Thus 45% of the victims in contact with the workers received crime prevention advice. Least advice was given to victims of violence. Either the workers felt there was nothing the victims could have done or the victim and assailant were known to each other and the workers did not feel crime prevention advice was appropriate for these types of incidents.

With regard to burglary victims, 19% (8) of the burgled households took the advice of the workers and made their own flats more secure. For the rest, either the council replaced their doors (9) or where the householders could not afford to make the necessary improvements themselves, the workers organised financial assistance and NACRO to carry out a security survey and improvements. A total of 38 flats had their security improvements paid for by the project (not all were burglary victims). The cost of materials to improve security ranged from £40 to £148.

Table 3

Crime prevention advice to victims (n = 154)

Crime	Advice Given	Advice Not Given	No. of victims
Burglary	40	2	42
Burglary artifice	12	—	12
Theft	5	11	17
Theft from car	3	7	10
Theft of car	2	3	5
Criminal damage	1	17	18
Arson	2	5	7
Rape	—	2	2
Indecent Exposure	—	2	2
Wounding	—	4	4
Assault	—	22	22
Threats	—	2	2
Street Robbery	2	6	8
Theft Person	2	2	4
TOTAL	69	85	154

Lessons Learned

(i)   Identifying victims

Although victims of reported and unreported crime and harassment on the estate did not readily come forward and ask for help, this was not an indication that they did not want any assistance even for what appeared to be minor crimes. It seems that a pro-active role by victim support workers to seek out victims is an important, but time-consuming, part of victim support work in inner city areas. The workers found victims were frequently out which probably reflected the fact they were often young and repeatedly calling at victims' homes took up a notable proportion of the workers' time. But when contact was finally made it seemed to be valued by the victims.

Given victims do not usually come forward themselves, it may be helpful to work from as many 'sources' of referral as possible. One such source is the police incident logs. In the first year of the project 60% of the potential crime incidents and 3% of the social disorder incidents reported to the police were subsequently recorded as crimes (see table 4).

Not all the no-crimed incidents will have had identifiable victims but most of the informants lived at the address of the incident (50%) or were neighbours (27%).

9

The impact of these incidents on the informants were likely to have been greater than if they had just been a passer-by witnessing an incident. Thus it is likely that incident logs are an important source of referral and given the total number in one year was 343 (almost twice as many incidents as recorded crime), they are an effective way to identify more victims and give crime prevention advice. Other 'sources' for example, may be social services departments and hospitals (Shepherd, 1988).

Table 4

Incident Log Data between 1st August 1988 and 31st July 1989

	Total no. of incidents	No. of 'crimed' incidents
1. Potential Crime		
Burglary (inc. attempts)	58	46
Suspects on premise	24	1
Theft (inc. M.V.)	23	23
Criminal Damage	24	24
Assault	41	12
Robbery	6	6
Drug taking	1	—
Rape	3	2
Threats	10	1
Arson	4	2
	194	117
2. Potential Disorder		
Accident/personal injury	8	1
Collapse/illness/drunk	16	—
Disturbance	79	3
Dispute	13	—
Complaint	33	—
	149	4

Note:
The layout of this table is based on table 3.7 in Shapland and Vagg (1988).

(ii) Providing crime prevention advice

A small number of victims received crime prevention advice. The workers sometimes felt advice was not always appropriate, especially where the victim and assailant were known to each other or the victim felt they had already taken every

10

possible precaution. There can be a fine line between giving crime prevention advice and blaming the victim, or discouraging residents from going out, both of which run counter to the aims of the project. For burglaries, only a few residents (19%) acted on crime prevention advice. A similar proportion to residents in an owner occupier area (Laycock, 1989), suggesting that there are reasons, beyond financial and protection of property, why people act or not.

(iii) The need for additional advice

When residents did come to the office it was not usually crime related; the majority of visitors wanted assistance and information on a wide range of issues. Table 5 gives a breakdown of the reasons. A small number of mainly elderly residents (approximately 15) frequently called in just for a chat and a cup of tea. These visits were not recorded.

Table 5

Reasons why residents visited the office

Reason for visit	Number of visits
Information/Advice/Assistance	
– financial advice (inc. debts/pensions)	24
– attendance at court/information on suspects	19
– neighbour disputes	14
– injunctions	8
– escort service by workers (to police station, hospital, shopping, to cash pensions)	9
– criminal compensation forms	5
– general information (not crime-related)	47
Sub-total	**126**
Housing problems	
– repairs (including block and street lighting)	51
– rehousing	16
– rent arrears	8
Sub-total	**75**
Crime Prevention	
– enquiries about progress of NACRO work	17
– enquiries about progress of work on intercom	16
– enquiries about the council's high security doors	4
– information sought on new locks	4
Sub-total	**41**
Crimes (see table 3 for further details)	
Sub-total	**50**
TOTAL	292

Note:
General information included a wide range of subjects including compensation on food poisoning, blood tests, vagrants, employment rights.

As table 5 indicates the project workers often acted as citizen advice bureau-type workers which required a wide range of knowledge about many different types of problems and led to regular contact with housing. By the end of two years the workers perceived their role as community workers specialising in victim support work. About 60% of their time was taken up responding to the immediate problems of residents. Where a victim support office is opened on an estate in deprived areas it would seem inevitable that workers will become involved in giving general help and assistance. The workers found it difficult to gain the trust of residents and one way their credibility increased was through their general advice activities. This benefitted their victim support/crime prevention work. However, the tensions between the general advice and information role and the victim support/crime prevention tasks were problematical, with the former becoming more and more time-consuming to the detriment of the latter.

One strategy which successfully reduced crime was adopted in the Kirkholt burglary prevention project. This was to target victims of repeat burglaries (Forrester et al, 1988, 1990). Whilst multi-victims accounted for just over a third of the reported crimes they were not just victims of repeat property crimes but of repeat personal crimes and some of both personal and property crimes. Where there were multi-burglary victims the solution seemed easier (the workers arranged for the council to fit high security doors to vulnerable locations). But the solutions for other types of multi-victims were less clear cut and indeed, repeat victimisation seemed in some instances to be symptomatic of deeper social and economic problems (Genn, 1988; Williams, 1983). The victim support work was not geared to giving special attention to multi-victims nor to giving long term support.

Summary of Lessons Learned

— victims did not usually come forward even though they wanted help. To achieve the aim of supporting all victims it will be necessary to identify them from more sources than recorded crime.

— the project workers became increasingly involved in citizen advice bureau-type work and this drew them away from victim-focused work.

— many victims needed financial assistance to make security improvements to their flats. Funding, therefore, needs to be available to projects.

— repeat victimisation accounted for almost a third of referrals from the police. However, a number of different types of response was required if the extent of multi-victimisation is to be reduced.

— crime prevention advice for some types of violent incidents (often where the victim and assailant are known to each other) can be inadequate. At least, victims can be advised on how to protect themselves.

Inter-Agency Working Group

The purpose of the working group was to assist in the implementation of the aims of the project and to deliver a more coordinated range of services to the estate. To assess the effectiveness of the working group, the content of the meetings, the decisions taken by the group, and 16 interviews with its members were analysed.

Table 6 shows there were 12 agencies represented on the working group with 19 members. The representatives of the social services, probation, transport police and tenants changed during the two years. The table also shows the attendance rate of the different agencies. In January 1990 participation was at an all time low; only victim support and the community social worker attended the meeting.

Table 6

Members and their attendance at working group meetings

Members	Number of meetings attended by at least one representative (n = 18)
Local victim support coordinator (chair)	18
Project worker	18
Project worker	16
Police (beat officer and community involvement officer)	15
Tenants' Association representative (three members)	14
CPU researcher	13
Social services community worker	12
Neighbourhood housing managers (two members)	11
NAVSS representative	9
Probation service (main grade officer)	8
Transport police (beat officer)	6
Local authority under 5s management representative	5
Representative from a neighbouring estate	3
Local authority police support unit (two members)	2

Notes:
1. For 10 of the meetings attended by the police there were at least two police officers present; for the 14 meetings attended by TA members, 12 were attended by at least two residents.
2. The transport police were invited to attend because there was a station on the perimeter of the estate.

At an informal level the time before and after the meetings provided the opportunity for exchanges of information and gossip which included reporting crimes to the police and discussing clients. At a formal level three phases can be identified in the evolution of the working group. The first meetings were dominated by information on the background to the project, results of the victimisation/crime prevention survey and the proposed aims. There was little comment by members and no objections were raised to the suggested aims. When domestic assaults and racial tensions were raised the tenants' representatives did not think these were a problem. As with other inter-agency groups, these remained 'silent' issues (Blagg et al, 1988), despite the findings of the victimisation survey.

The second phase in the evolution of the working group was precipitated by the survey results on incivilities and poor housing maintenance. This phase was marked by two different agendas. On the one hand there were the immediate concerns of the residents, typically about the car – either speeding, illegal dumping or disruptive parking – unruly children and youths, and 'problem' families. On the other agenda was the progress of the project, the difficulties faced by the workers in implementing the aims and how these problems might be resolved. Issues raised in both agendas often remained unresolved, or were resolved after a long period of time. For example, ideas for crime prevention not taken up included leaflets for new residents, property marking, showing a video to the elderly and the removal of graffiti by community service order clients. If there were any problems crucial to the continuation of the project then the chair of the group (the victim support coordinator) arranged a meeting or made a telephone call to senior management independently of the working group. Her numerous personal contacts were key channels through which things 'happened'. For example, meetings were held with senior police to try and resolve referral problems, and telephone calls were made to the senior housing personnel about the installation of the intercom system.

During the final six months the third phase became apparent. The dominant topic for discussion was the future of the project, the consequence for the residents if the workers withdrew, and how to continue the project when the funding finished. The immediate concerns of the residents were not raised and the progress of the project took a back seat. During this phase the main interest came from victim support, the police and the community social worker who attended all the meetings. The residents were supportive of the workers continuing and there was strong support for the continuation of an inter-agency initiative from the police.

These developments were discussed with 16 members of the group who were interviewed in March and April 1990 (1). They were asked about their role within the group and how it related to their own organisation, how they thought the group had performed and their views on the project.

Most of the interviews lasted well over an hour. Interviewees stressed the importance of inter-agency working and said they joined the group because it was 'part of their job'. Most members met each other for the first time at the initial meeting and

---

(1) The role of the local victim support management committee has not been discussed in this paper. The workers submitted reports to the committee on a regular basis but, apart from the support of the chair, they did not play an active part in the project.

felt it took a long time before agencies actually worked well together. In fact, the overwhelming majority had few expectations that the group would ever be more than a support group for the project workers.

With one exception, those interviewed felt their own work had benefited from information learned from other members of the group and they felt their clients had also benefited from this increased knowledge. Group members contacted each other outside the meetings. These contacts were mostly to exchange information about clients, or to ask for assistance. Two members helped on a police-run summer play scheme. Other beneficial effects included raising the profile of the estate, so that when it came to the allocation of resources by the local authority, the estate was given higher priority. The profile of crime prevention was also raised and, although for most agencies it was still given a low priority, the crime prevention work of the local victim support increased.

Except for supporting and advising the workers most group members were uncertain what their contribution to the meetings had been. Representatives of the statutory agencies, and in particular the local housing authority and the police, thought an important part of their role was to state the perspective of their agency and outline their statutory responsibilities and constraints on what they could do. Those who had either replaced a colleague or joined the group in the course of the two years were the least certain of their role and their contribution. This, uncertainty is by no means uncommon in groups of this kind (Sampson et al, 1988; Sampson and Smith, 1990; Geraghty, 1991).

Members' uncertainty about their role stemmed in part from the 'isolation' they felt in their own organisation. At least half of the statutory agency workers felt their own work was considered marginal within their own organisation and this credibility gap limited the importance given to the project. A few workers complained that they were not given the time by their senior managers to read the minutes, think through the problems or attend meetings. Where decisions were referred back to senior managers they either did not respond, or took over 6 months to come back with an answer.

The overwhelming majority of members raised the issue of conflict within the group, referred to one or two particular incidents and commented on how disruptive and unsettling they had found it because they did not understand 'what was going on'. Conflicts between group members were indicative of 'hidden' agendas and the feeling that members were not being given the 'whole story' about the future of the project.

Another common complaint was that the members felt the Home Office and NAVSS usurped their decision-making power. There was also ambiguity about the relationship between the working group and the management of the workers. Members felt the workers made their own decisions and did not take up their suggestions; for example, setting up a property marking scheme or giving advice to new residents who were more likely than established residents to be burgled (CPU paper 21). The majority of the working group thought they should have had some management responsibilities for the workers.

Lessons Learned

It is apparent that there were substantial shortcomings in the intended catalytic role of the working group to forward the aims of the project which suggests a different inter-agency structure may have been more effective. This section proposes an alternative model.

(i)   Power and responsibility

The working group provided the workers with support and advice but it was essentially powerless. They felt that NAVSS/CPU interests and demands would override their decisions. As a result the working group never really took any responsibility for the implementation of the aims.

Engendering joint ownership of a project requires decision-making power. Early involvement would increase the working group's sense of ownership; increase the residents' awareness of the scheme; help minimise rumours and gossip; and assist in building a rapport between the residents and the project workers. It was also apparent that the project workers needed to have some accountability to the working group, to enhance its authority. This would not exclude the day-to-day management of the workers by one agency, in this instance, victim support but if there is a 'lead' agency responsible for the project and its workers, difficulties arise. When there are problems the other agencies tend to distance themselves and say "it's not my problem", and take no action.

(ii) Membership

Membership of the group is clearly important. It will need to be able to manage conflict between its members constructively and to deal with the agenda-setting capacity of the more powerful agencies at the expense of the less powerful. A small 'core' working group with approximately six members may be more suitable for a multi-agency approach (provided there are few dominant agencies who form this core group). In this project a core group could have been the tenants' association (two members), victim support (two project workers and local coordinator), the community social worker, and the local neighbourhood housing manager.

The core working group could then invite other agencies to attend meetings where the agenda is appropriate to their tasks. This would ensure invited agencies had a clear role and a contribution to make. For example the local under 5s management team could be invited to help and advise drawing up a constitution for the mothers' and toddlers' group, the firebrigade to advise on reducing fire escapes used by offenders as escape routes, police to comment on crime trends, or the probation service asked for help from clients on community service orders to paint out graffiti. So that decisions affecting the progress of the project can be made at meetings and their implications discussed with the decision-makers, two people from each agency could be invited to a working group meeting, one senior manager and one grassroots worker.

(iii) Timing of meetings

Members of the working group found it easier to work with people they knew and felt the group would have achieved a better working relationship if they had got to know each other quicker. Accordingly, a series of frequent meetings, say 4 in a month, at the start of the project, followed by monthly meetings, may enable a group to develop more effective relationships early on. Otherwise issues raised are not thoroughly discussed (this happened, for example, with residents' reservations about care watch).

(iv) Agenda setting and minutes

Setting the agenda is important for the development of the project. There will be continuous tension between setting out and achieving its aims and responding to more immediate problems of the residents which can 'blow up' – for example a spate of fires in residents' letter boxes and in rubbish shutes, and children playing on roof tops. Space on an agenda to discuss, and if possible respond, to these problems will give the project more credibility with the residents. Room could also be given to invited agencies to raise issues they think are important. Full and accurate minutes of the meetings proved essential when there was disagreement between agencies. They were useful as points of reference during arguments. When possible an 'outsider' might be the most preferable minute writer.

(v) The chair

Members thought the coordinator of victim support was the right person to chair the meetings and they were satisfied by the way in which she carried out this task. The chair has to juggle several roles and, perhaps, not enough attention has been given to recognising these skills. Specific training may be necessary to achieve a more effective inter-agency group. The members of any group are unlikely to have many interests in common and coping with these differences is a task for the chair. The research findings highlighted the importance of directly, and openly, dealing with this conflict, otherwise trust between members of the group can be undermined and uncertainties about hidden agendas may develop. The chair also has to stimulate practical action. Most members of a group will already be overworked and their agencies probably under-resourced. In these circumstances getting commitment requires considerable skills.

The findings on the inter-agency group suggest that through informal communication a more co-ordinated delivery of services was beginning to emerge but that the group did not make a notable impact on implementating the aims. Its role was primarily one of support and advice to the project workers. An alternative model of working has been suggested with a 'core' membership of not more than six members and other agencies invited to particular meetings. A series of meetings close together at the start of a project, the fostering of joint responsibility, and a chair skillful at managing conflict, are all cited as important elements to this model.

Summary of Lessons Learned

— a working group set up to assist in the implementation of a crime prevention project needs

    i) to be informed about crime prevention advice and know how to give crime prevention assistance.
    ii) to have power to make decisions
    iii) to be a body to which the project workers are accountable.

— in the initial stages a few meetings in quick succession would assist towards the forming of a working relationship between group members.

— the management of conflicts between the preoccupations and interests of local agencies and residents may be more effective if there is a 'core' working group of about 6 members, which would invite other agencies to attend specified meetings.

— the lack of cooperation from powerful agencies may impede the progress of a project. Their role needs to be carefully considered.

— group members marginal to their own organisation, and without influence, are unable to commit their agency to any changes in working practices or policy. The involvement of senior managers may be necessary to overcome these difficulties.

— tension between aims of the project and current problems of the residents was a recurring theme and to maintain credibility, some of the immediate problems of residents need to be addressed.

— full and accurate minutes of meetings can be helpful in disputes between agencies.

Care Watch

Care watch was similar in concept to the cocoon neighbourhood watch on the Kirkholt estate where neighbours were asked to 'wrap round' a victim to protect them from further victimisation (Forrester et al, 1988, 1990). In addition care watch met the project's objective of encouraging self-help and setting up long term support networks for victims. One possible effect of care watch was the potential to reduce fear of strangers and engender a feeling of safety. When the workers visited neighbours of a victim to set up a care watch they were also to give them crime prevention advice. In the event, care watches were not implemented. The two most probable reasons for this were either care watch was not acceptable to the residents and/or the workers were not able to 'sell' the idea and persuade residents to join.

The following discussion of these possibilities are based on 27 in-depth interviews with victims which typically lasted for at least an hour and a half. In six interviews a partner or friend was present. The interview schedules were semi-structured and the questions adapted several times to incorporate issues that arose in previous interviews. All the interviews took place six months after the incident had been reported to the workers (see Appendix for further details). Information from at least 40 other victims and residents also contributed to the points made below.

There was little doubt that most victims welcomed the assistance given to them by the workers, particularly if they were able to solve practical problems, for example, help to fill in criminal compensation forms, obtain injunctions, sort out insurance problems, have urgent housing repairs done, or to get information from the police, the courts or solicitors relevant to their incident. The interviewed victims were also appreciative of the emotional support provided by the workers; 'it's nice to know there's someone like you who cares', was a usual comment.

Whilst all those interviewed thought there was a role for victim support on the estate, the findings suggest that support for such work between the residents themselves was patchy (for similar findings see Bulmer, 1986). Such inter-neighbour support as did exist was limited to a few isolated pockets of friendly neighbouring and this proved difficult to extend to other neighbours. Perhaps the most important reason for this was the strong sense of privacy held by many residents. Victims usually told their neighbours about what had happened (except for burglary artifice incidents) but it was in a passing conversation on the landing or on the street.

Only three interviewed victims were unequivocally in favour of care watch (as it happens, three victims who were not seen by the workers). There was however a widespread recognition of the benefits of neighbouring, usually expressed in terms of increased feelings of security.

I think I get a lot of security by knowing the people who live in the block (Victim in her 20s).

We used to have nice neighbours ... they were friendly. We all kept to ourselves but we all kept an eye on each other ... It makes you feel secure, you know who's living there and you know you can trust them (Victim in her 30s).

19

Among those not prepared to participate in care watch, 89% (24) said their reservations over-rode these perceived advantages. The remainder of this section discusses some of the obstacles to supportive neighbouring experienced by the interviewed victims.

From the perspective of caring, victims' concerns were mostly about life styles and age differences. The following comments give a flavour of the reluctances (for similar findings see Newman, 1981):

> There's a young fellow underneath. I have nothing to do with him. I wouldn't go to him. He wouldn't understand old women's problems. (Victim in her 60s).

> I'd love to have close neighbours like I did when I first moved in. Next door is an ex-mental patient living in appalling conditions [and opposite] some young girls. They change all the time. I don't know who's there and who's not. They give off a feeling of hostility and don't talk to me (Victim in her 40s).

A woman victim in her 20s summed up the sentiments of those who actually distrusted some of their immediate neighbours (44%) and were, therefore, reluctant to offer each other emotional support.

> I don't think people want to take too much responsibility... People don't give up things easily and certainly don't give up their privacy. They don't make big friendship gestures at all. People hold on pretty tight. It's an alien environment that's changing all the time and it's not in their control. They can't even get very basic things like messes in the hallway cleared... On a day-to-day level like buying food and acknowledging people's existance I think its alright but you scratch the surface and I think there are some pretty horrible attitudes. Its not just black/white, there's a lot of fighting. That's another reason why people keep themselves to themselves because you get over-involved (Victim in her 20s).

The feeling of living in an 'alien environment' seemed to reinforce residents notions of privacy. Except for domestic attacks, victims perceived their flats as a safe haven compared to the outside world; 'I never relax until I've shut that front-door' or 'I'm in a state of high alert until the door is shut' were typical comments. This discouraged interaction between neighbours in communal areas of the blocks and created feelings of distance and isolation.

Thus one of the fundamental objections to care watch by victims was allowing many of their neighbours into their flats. Only six of those interviewed let their neighbours visit regularly. Three were in the same block and offered each other emotional support and three were elderly residents whose neighbours bought them a daily newspaper or did any 'emergency' shopping or just 'checked up on them'. Where neighbours were offering each other emotional support they seemed to be of similar age and share similar circumstances; there was, for example, one group of widows, one of retired people and another of mothers with young children. Otherwise the most common type of help between neighbours was utilitarian which might be built on and encouraged but is quite different to the emotional support given to victims by victim support workers.

Instead of turning to neighbours all the victims with family nearby (13) turned to them as 'trusted' people for emotional, practical and sometimes financial support after they had been victimised. This was a natural extention to the frequent contact and help given between family members, which included regular visiting, doing each others shopping and washing, sharing child care and looking after elderly parents. Interestingly these victims still tended to require practical help from the workers who used the 'authority' of the victim support organisation, and their specialist skills, to try and solve practical problems. It seemed unlikely that residents helping themselves would be able to achieve as much.

Another aspect of care watch was that neighbours would 'watch out' for each other. In all but one case victims watched out for some of their neighbours and thought their neighbours were watching for them. However, from the perspective of crime prevention, first the victimisation survey and then the interviews with victims cast some doubts on watching as an effective burglary reduction measure, even where there was some evidence of social cohesion (Sampson and Farrell, 1990). Of the 12 interviews which discussed watching and its implications in detail, one victim thought watching prevented crime whereas everyone else thought 'it might do up to a point' or it was 'unlikely to' but thought the benefit of watching, and being watched, was an increased sense of security (these views were widely held by other residents as well). At first sight this appears to contradict the finding of 'distrust' between neighbours. However, watching seemed to be an activity that did not demand much personal involvement between neighbours and indeed, 'watchers' were often reluctant to get involved if they did not observe something 'suspicious'. There seemed to be a supposition that watching was happening but victims were not always sure by whom. It typically seemed to take place between small numbers of residents (2 or 3 households) so that they did not watch for everyone in the same block. Only where neighbours were actually friends, or where victims thought their neighbours were 'nosey', did neighbours feedback what they had seen or heard, including information about who had visited them whilst they were out.

On the face of it there appeared to be scope to develop watching so neighbours knew who in their block was actually watching, and to include those who were not. But those who had reservations about care watch (89%) had two particular comments about the 'watching'. One set of objections was that since there was already informal watching, there was no need to formalise the system through care watch. Taking on more responsibility was also associated with formalised watching which victims did not appear to want. A victim, who was already watching her neighbour's flat, but was against care watch said 'If I was care watching someone's flat and they got burgled I'd feel terrible'. The workers found it difficult to persuade victims, on the basis of these objections, to press for the formalisation of watching. Where there was no watching, they found it even harder because victims often actively distrusted their neighbours.

A difficulty with the concept of care watch was the idea that intervention on the part of the watcher was necessary to deter criminals and to stop anti-social behaviour. For a number of reasons residents were reluctant to do this. The image of watching was, for some, incompatible with estate life:

> Neighbourhood watch smacks of something the estate is not. It smacks of the street across the road. Big houses and big cars. Neighbourhood watch is about the middle-class looking over middle class goods... It's also a bit of a joke if no one is going to challenge the kids, they're certainly not going to challenge adults. That's a major problem here ... (Victim in her 20s).

Another victim reiterates the feelings of intimidation neighbours feel about intervening.

> Years ago you could just knock on the door and say please could you turn down your radio or please could you be a bit quieter. But now you can't do that. It's too dangerous. The men and women give you a load of abuse and threaten to come at you ... The atmosphere feels very unpleasant at times (Victim in her 50s).

Retaliation if an incident was reported to the police was also a difficulty, and one which was felt particularly by active officers of the tenants' association. Four committee members felt they had been intimidated in one three month period because they'd called the police to various incidents of disorder. Other residents commented:

> I know Mr M [a neighbour] is not prepared to do that [call the police to a disturbance] 'cos he's got a motor car out there and he's afraid, with the sort of people around now, they might damage it. It's fear of reprisals that's what it is (Resident in her 60s).

In discussions with those who had lived on the estate for the last 20 to 30 years five out of six victims spontaneously recalled the role caretakers played in the upkeep of the estate and in maintaining social order:

> Mr Dots never let the estate get this bad. He was wonderful. He kept the shutes clean, did the lights. If there was a noise he'd tell people. If kids from another estate played on the swings, he's send them packing (Victim in her 60s).

The attitudes of the workers were also important at the implementation stage. Initially they were both supportive and enthusiastic about the idea of care watch and thought it possible. However they soon picked up the victims' reservations and became sympathetic to their objections. One of the workers lived on a similar near-by estate and felt 'it was an invasion of privacy' asking victims in a confidential meeting if they could approach their neighbours at a time when they were upset. This view was supported by the other worker. They found that victims sometimes did not want their neighbours to know they had been victimised and felt their loyalties were primarily to the victim, not to the achievement of the aims of the project.

Lessons Learned

Early on in the project the workers picked up the victims' reservations about care watch and became unenthusiastic about implementing this aim. It could be argued that because the workers were not committed to 'selling' care watch, care watches were not implemented. The findings suggest, however, even with workers committed to the idea and skilful at persuading residents, care watches were unlikely to have gained widespread support.

The reluctance of neighbours to become too involved with each other's personal lives, distrust and sometimes open hostility, disapproval of different life-styles, and their consequent notions of privacy and unwillingness to let neighbours visit their flats were all obstacles to 'caring' between neighbours (see also Newman, 1981). Where neighbours were supportive of each other they appeared to share a common interest and encouraging such support (the idea behind the mothers' and toddlers' group), may be a more effective way to foster self-help between victims.

The experiences of the workers suggest that without some extra 'authority' and knowledge, victims and neighbours would not be able to overcome as many of the practical problems as the workers. For example, providing information about what is happening to their case and giving support in court (see table 5; also Newburn and Merry, 1990). Other changes to make a less 'alien' environment would appear to be necessary conditions for the fostering of neighbourliness, but such substantive changes would be beyond the current responsibilities of victim support workers.

Although watching was a widespread activity (a similar finding to Shapland and Vagg, 1988), victims' multi-dimensional fears and feelings of vulnerability made them reluctant to tackle problems of anti-social behaviour and suspicious 'happenings' themselves. Tackling some of these fears may have been a necessary precursor to an effective implementation of care watch and for 'watching' to be a successful crime reduction activity.

Summary of Lessons Learned

— there were strong disincentives to participating in care watch and these 'fears' needed to be tackled before many residents would consider joining.

— distrust and sometimes intimidation between residents needed to be overcome before participation in care watch would have been forthcoming. Community mediation is a possible solution.

— emotionally supportive neighbours had common interests and it is therefore possible that developing community organisations would increase support between residents in the same neighbourhood.

— victims greatest concern was for their safety – in both public and private places – and improvements to increase their security were important for gaining the confidence of residents in the project.

— residents did not feel they could tackle anti-social behaviour on their own and therefore wanted assistance from local agencies.

— victims often could not solve their practical problems on their own and required the 'authority' and skills of the victim support workers.

— the commitment of workers to a project's aims is important because 'selling' a strategy to residents and agencies is crucial.

— if residents' resistances to a preventive strategy become well-founded, changing aims is always an option.

Block Watch

Residents found strangers in their block menacing, felt safe only when they were in their own flats and were reluctant to exchange more than a brief word in the communal areas. Furthermore, it was found that watching out for each others flats did not in itself engender neighbouring or a community spirit. These findings suggested communual security may be one prerequisite for increased neighbourliness since this would give residents a safe communal area within which to interact.

Police crime prevention officers advised that an intercom system was more reliable in small blocks of flats where fewer users could abuse the system. The workers decided to ask residents in a small, poorly maintained block how safe they felt in their own flat and in the communal areas and how they thought their safety could be improved. 22 out of the 24 households were interviewed and they all said that they were most afraid in the communal areas and they would like an intercom system or communal security doors. The residents were less enthusiastic about a formal system of blockwatching with a coordinator. Either they thought it was not necessary because they already had an informal system of watching or they were not interested. They were more enthusiastic after they were told it was a 'condition' of having an intercom system installed. Table 7 gives a brief history of its installation.

It took ten months for victim support and housing to agree on the type of communal security and it was 16 months before the job was completed. A number of the problems encountered are worth noting. As other estate-based projects have experienced, getting residents to attend meetings is particularly difficult (Safe Neighbourhoods Unit, undated). Where there are small numbers of households, in this case 24, the workers found it easier just to visit each household seperately rather than make a time-consuming effort to arrange a meeting which few people attended.

At the inter-agency working group meetings in May and June 1989 block watches were discussed but it was not until the July meeting that the housing department said they had not been properly consulted and complained that the residents had not taken the decision back to the tenants' association. By this time the residents of the block had already agreed with the workers on the type of communal security they preferred. The problem was that the housing neighbourhood officers could not give approval for the intercom to be installed and they had not consulted other departments within the council. As a result the programme was delayed three months until the appropriate meetings had been held, and permission was given.

Another delay occured due to the lengthy negotiations between the victim support workers and the local authority housing department about what type of intercom system should be installed and who was responsible for the maintenance of the system. The council's construction department repeatedly failed to turn up to meetings arranged to discuss the installation. A quote was then obtained from a private company but housing refused to maintain the proposed system because it did not comply with their own specifications. The council's argument was that the proposed system was not vandal-proof. To construct a system to the council standards made it prohibitively expensive for victim support to consider. In the end a compromise was reached. Victim support obtained two more quotes and accepted one for £8,000 compared to £4,500 for the original quotation and £37,000 for the one laid down by council requirements. The company was to carry out 'normal' maintenance to the system for a year after they had installed it and victim support was to pay for any damage caused by vandalism for the first year. Thereafter the council would take over this responsibility.

The concerns of the representatives of the tenants' association on the working group were quite different to the housing department. Their preoccupation was that a 'problem family', as they called them, lived in the block where the intercom was to be installed and they felt that this family would abuse the system and make it difficult to encourage any neighbourliness. The residents also thought it unlikely that the intercom system would modify the behaviour of this family who intimidated their neighbours, but were willing to 'see what happened'.

Table 7

History of the installation of the intercom system.

Date (month/year)	Action Required	Outcome
May 1989	Choose a block of flats	Small block (24 hholds) chosen by the workers
June 1989	Residents' views on communal security	22 hholds in favour of communal security
June 1989	Funding	Obtained from Research and Statistical Dept.
July 1989	Type of security acceptable to residents.	Consensus amongst residents on intercom system
	Housing dept. demand more consultation and ask the TA to take intercom plan to their committee	Meetings held in September
Sept. 1989	Project workers to obtain quotes for work	4 meetings cancelled by council construction dept. Quote obtained from private company
Dec. 1989	Discuss timetable for installation with residents	2 meetings held and due to poor attendance the workers visited each household
	Council objected to quality of intercom system. New quote required	Quote obtained to council specifications was £37,000 (Original quote was for £4,500)
Feb. 1990	Council specifications too expensive for project to undertake	Police crime prevention officer survey flats. Compromise reached between housing and victim support on intercom specifications
	New quotes necessary	Quote for £8,000 accepted from a private company in March
May 1990	Council to upgrade doors before intercom work can finish	
Sept. 1990	Intercom installed	

Lessons Learned

The negotiations with the local housing authority to install the security hardware were difficult, conflictual and time consuming. They may have been easier if the working group had been more directive and agreed a timetable of work with housing in writing. The purpose of such action would have been to counter the powerful position of the local authority department who were able to delay, and even prevent, the installation of the intercom system.

It became apparent that members of the working group, in this case from housing, did not always fully absorb the implications of decisions made for their own agency in an inter-agency setting. This was more likely to happen when members missed meetings. With hindsight, it would have been worth asking housing exactly what steps had to be taken, and by whom, within their agency to ensure the installation of the intercom system within a reasonable time period. Understanding the internal management structure identifies key personnel who have the authority to make the necessary decisions. The importance of clear and full minutes of inter-agency meetings has already been noted. During the course of several negotiations between housing and victim support the minutes were used to support or refute positions.

A different set of lessons were learned about vandalism. A number of difficult decisions were necessary about how vandal-proof the system should be. Victim support questioned the necessity of some of the local authority's specifications and their high installation costs. To reach a compromise the project workers prioritised certain vandal proof features and found a company with cheaper installation costs. Another problem was the issue of repairs to the system damaged by vandals. The council insisted that victim support were responsible for this during the first year of operation. Budgetting for the cost of vandalism is practically impossible and the financial risks may be too high for a small locally-based initiative.

Finally, the adverse effect some families had on other residents living in the same block of flats became clear. The complaints about these families were numerous, usually stretched over a long period of time and were often vehemently expressed. Whilst most were accused of criminal and anti-social behaviour, they were also victims and known to the project workers. For these reasons a victims support/crime prevention scheme cannot easily side-step this issue of 'problem' families, a phenomena which seems common to many high density inner-city dwellings (Wilson, 1963; Bottoms and Wiles, 1986; Reynolds, 1986; Power, 1989).

Summary of Lessons Learned

— residents were most concerned about their safety in the communal areas in their block of flats. This should be considered at the same time as the security of individual dwellings.

— residents were willing in principle to incorporate 'difficult' families into a communal security system, but it remains to be seen how this works out in practice.

— a formal agreement with the local housing department on the timetable for the installation of a security system was necessary.

— vandalism – how vandal proof should the security improvements be? and who pays for the damage? – were particularly important issues on which to agree at an early stage.

Mothers and Toddlers Group

It was thought that in a group setting residents would be encouraged to report crimes, it would be an opportunity to give crime prevention advice and support victims (nearly half the children under 5 years old lived in blocks of flats with higher crime; new residents were more frequently burgled than established households; and mothers were likely to be new residents (Sampson and Farrell, 1990)) and the process of networking and friendship could be encouraged between residents with a common interest. Of all the aims and activities there was the most positive support for a mothers' and toddlers' group, from members of the working group and from mothers with young children. Yet the implementation difficulties were not overcome and the group had a short and strife-ridden life. A brief resume of its history (table 8) illustrates the main problems.

Most of the different tensions and problems experienced during the course of the project were exemplified and intensified in the rise and demise of the mothers' and toddlers' group. First, there was an ambiguous relationship between the mothers and the project workers, in part because the mothers started the group independently of the workers. The workers did not want to take a directive role in managing the group because the project was only scheduled to run for two years, but they did want to assist in its day-to-day management and introduce crime prevention education into the activities. The workers attended the twice weekly play sessions but by the time a management committee was set up the conflicts over the use of the TA flat had galvanised the mothers into an angry and defensive group who perceived other groups (for example, the management committee) as threatening and intrusive. This made the workers relations with the mothers even more ambiguous.

Secondly, the intra-tenants' association tensions (there were four different chairs due to votes of no confidence during the two years) manifested themselves as angry conflict about the use of their flat by the mothers' and toddlers' group. One faction of the TA accused the mothers' and toddlers' group of making too much noise, the ill-treatment of children, leaving the flat and the area outside a mess, and degrading the estate by having a jumble sale at their play meetings. Another supported the mothers' and toddlers' group using the TA flat. The workers were perceived by the anti-mothers' and toddlers' group as supporting the mothers, after they tried to mediate between the two groups. A formerly friendly relationship between the former group of residents and the workers turned into ambivalence.

Table 8

History of the mothers' and toddlers' group.

Date	Significant Events/Decisions
Nov. 1988	Accepted as an aim by the working group. Insurance necessary. Grant for £100 obtainable from social services.
Dec. 1988	5 mothers started group in church hall. Met with project workers and social services to discuss funding and the constitution. Working group discussed obtaining a portacabin which was on offer for free.
Jan. 1989	Officially opened by well-known first division football player.
Feb. 1989	Church hall too expensive. Moved to tenants' association (TA) flat.
March 1989	Insurance situation uncertain. Friction with members of the TA. No decision made on portacabin and it was given away to another group. Project workers helped with constitution.
April 1989	Cannot afford electricity. Efforts made by working group to find another portacabin. Attendance rate increased from 10 to 15 mothers.
June 1989	Residents complain about noise, mess, and the jumble for sale outside the TA flat. Project workers coopted onto newly formed management committee. Constitution accepted. Group can apply for funds. Second-hand portacabin, free of charge, found.
July 1989	Dispute between mothers and toddlers management committee and the TA. Housing to obtain planning permission and arrange site for portacabin.
Sept. 1989	Voted out of TA flat. Moved back to church hall. Attendance low. Received £100 grant from social services. Housing had not applied for planning permission and looked for storage space for portacabin.
Oct. 1989	Dispute between 'original' mothers. Mothers' and toddlers' group all but ceased.
Dec. 1989	Portacabin burned down. Dispute about who should remove the charred remains.

Thirdly, the problems the working group had in galvanising slow moving bureaucracies into action were well-illustrated. It took 11 months before social services came up with a grant for the group, by which time it was all but disbanded. Housing never did sort out the planning permission for the portacabin and for two months it was left on the estate to be commissioned before it was burned down.

A final important issue was the recurring discussion about who was going to own and manage the community activities based in the portacabin. The TA representatives did not want one group, i.e., the mothers' and toddlers', monopolising its use. Although victim support did not want to manage the use of the portacabin, they did not want the TA to be the sole users and prevent others from using it, as they had done with the TA flat. Eventually, after a number of informal deputations to the project workers by the TA and housing, it was decided victim support would set up a management committee and, until it was well-established, manage the activities. Even though none of this happened because the portacabin was burned down it illustrated the kind of debate that which may take place at the implementation phase of any community development initiative.

Lessons Learned

This project has illustrated how crime prevention schemes can increase social conflicts and provide a site for power struggles to be played out. Negotiating an agreement between conflicting groups is, as the history of this project clearly illustrates, often essential for the implementation of a crime prevention strategy. Some ways in which this conflict can be made more manageable are, for example; to undertake initial groundwork, particularly on the dynamics of the TA; to anticipate some reactions to new activities; to decide on the boundaries of the project and the limits of their involvement as a guidance to the workers, and a working group; and to keep expectations as realistic as possible, which can be achieved, in part, by giving residents clear and up-to-date information. One mistake, which misled residents, was to show some pictures of new portacabins at a working group meeting. When the second-hand one arrived they felt let down and were criticised by other residents. This undermined their role as representatives of the TA and did nothing to enhance their relations with the project workers.

Another difficulty, not unique to this project, is that residents often lack management and administrative skills to set up a group and sustain its activities and membership (Knight and Hayes, 1981; Podolefsky and DuBow, 1981). A training programme is therefore often required for leaders of a group. There is also a question as to whether groups should remain voluntarily run or be organised by paid workers. These issues are beyond the scope of this paper but they lead back to a more relevant question about the involvement of victim support in setting up community infrastructures and overtly pursuing a community development role in conjunction with their casework. Both tasks require quite different skills and expertise.

The lack of any formal community infrastructure made it particularly difficult to start a community group. Choosing an estate with existing organised activities would have been a distinct advantage as the workers could have liaised with these groups from the perspective of supporting victims and giving crime prevention advice, not with a broader agenda as instigators of a group.

Summary of Lessons Learned

— residents may need book keeping and administration training to run a community group.

— efforts made to keep residents' expectations realistic about what can be achieved, will assist the implementation phase.

— where community development is part of the aims of a project having some existing organisations to tap into is likely to provide an easier 'starting point' for the initiative.

— crime prevention projects can provide a site for power struggles between agencies and residents which may need to be directly confronted and mediated by the project leader or coordinator.

Community Mediation

Once community mediation was accepted as an aim, primarily to resolve neighbour disputes, it was decided to work with an independent local mediation service so that the workers would be properly trained, insured and supported. The victim support coordinator joined the steering committee of the proposed service which was borough-wide and launched in Februay 1990. In the first 5 months this scheme received 73 referrals 35, of which were from local authority housing estates (including two from the project estate). Most of the referrals were self-referrals (71%).

Although neighbour disputes were not studied in any great detail a number of observations are worth noting. Where there was a recurring dispute, which many were, they affected most of the other residents living in the same block of flats. At the research interviews, victims often raised the issue of neighbour disputes spontaneously. Principally they were frightened during the dispute and aware that it could escalate so that they may, unwittingly, become involved and get hurt. Although disputes erupted into damage against property from time to time, they were often accompanied by ongoing unfriendliness and petty aggravations that served as continuous reminders of the antagonisms.

Thus, although the actual number of disputes might be small their knock-on effects can be substantial, for example, 2 disputes affected 48 households. Everyone in the block took sides and this created anxieties. Successful resolution at an early stage of a neighbour dispute can prevent a general escalation of violent outbursts. It seems possible that a dispute resolution service might also reduce fears of residents which emanate from feelings of vulnerability arising from neighbour disputes.

Concluding Comments

The notion of a community development approach to preventing crime has not been undermined by the project's limited success. It took place on an estate where there were a multitude of problems which required intervention on a much larger scale than could be undertaken by the victim support/crime prevention initiative. This problem aside, it is possible that the estate is 'typical' of other local authority housing estates where there is a hetereogenous population living in flats in a deprived inner-city area. This estate stands in contrast to Kikholt where there was a successful burglary prevention initiative (Forrester et al., 1988, 1990) and which is located on the edge of a town, is mostly houses and has an all white population with one substantive type of crime problem, namely burglary. Crime prevention packages clearly need to be adapted to different types of estate.

There seemed to be three particularly important characteristics of the estate in the victim support/crime prevention project relevant to a crime prevention inititive. First there was no one predominant crime; there was a fairly even distribution between a wide range of property and personal offences. There was 'not enough' of one type of crime on which to target and make a significant preventive impact (this was crime which came to the attention of the project workers – much of the domestic and racial crimes remained 'hidden' (CPU paper 21)). For example, there were 47 incidents of reported burglary for the first year of the project, on an estate with 33 blocks of flats. Repeat victimisation was identified as a problem but it was not clear how multi-victims (other than burglary) could be helped. This was particularly the case where the assailant and victim were known to each other (62% of the personal incidents in the victimisation survey). In addition, youths who repeatedly fought in the street required a different preventative response to domestic attacks or neighbour assaults.

A second important feature was the multi-dimensional nature of residents' fears. Their lives were blighted by social conflicts and tensions. Some of these conflicts reflected divisions between gender, race, and age while others were about divergent life-styles, divisions between the employed and unemployed, disparate values and the use of space on the estate. These differences engendered significant resistances to care watches, improved neighbouring and more effective social control between neighbours and their children (see also Newman, 1981). The fear of being attacked was found to be widespread, and for women this was a fear of sexual attack (Sampson and Farrell, 1990). The interviews with burglary victims showed that fears about burglary were also fears of being personally harmed. Living in run-down high density housing contributed to these 'fears'. Isolation seemed to be another source of anxiety. Two victims summed up some of the feelings about living in flats.

> A flat has to do with crime. In flats you don't have to pass people's front doors. You don't come into contact with people so much. People living above each other can be very irritating (Victim in her 70s).

> I am very lonely ... I got no friends on the estate ... I used to sit outside the street door and people would pass and have a chat. The next-door neighbour would make a pot of tea one afternoon and I'd make it the next. But here you don't see nobody (Victim in her 80s).

The reactions to these types of conflicts and tensions took two main forms; one, to fight back and the other, to withdraw defensively. Since these reactions arose largely from feelings of vulnerability and distrust, it would seem necessary to have a preventive strategy that aimed to acknowledge the fears of the residents.

A third characteristic was the lack of prompt and effective response from statutory agencies which compounded residents' problems. The statutory and voluntary agencies in the locality were over-stretched and protective of their own autonomy. Historically there were some long running disputes of a political nature between the agencies (as well as being task orientated (Sampson et al., 1988)). As a result the workers found it difficult to tap into networks to establish a cooperative base from which to work.

In addition to these three characteristics, which illustrated that any effective intervention had to be substantive, there were at least four further elements to the project which can be identified as having an important influence on its outcome.

First, the significant role of funds for the implementation of crime prevention strategies was clearly illustrated. Giving crime prevention advice to improve security went largely unheeded until the workers had funds to organise, and pay for, the necessary improvements which were beyond the means of most residents. Residents were more receptive to block watch, and willing to bury their own differences, when it was clear there were funds for individual and communal security improvements. The project gained credibility through their ability to offer practical help to victims and the workers had a more visible role and could see tangible results. Moreover those victims who were helped practically seemed then to have the space to work through their emotional upset. Without this practical help it was as though victims' emotional upheavals, and sometimes, anger, lingered on and contributed to the 'high temperature' of the estate. These impressions of continuing emotional turmoil are supported by other studies (Shapland et al, 1985; Maguire and Corbett, 1987; Marshall, 1990).

Secondly, was the role of victim support as a 'lead' agency and their involvement in community development. The skills required for community work are quite different to those necessary to support victims, and the activities of the project workers illustrated how victims did not necessarily remain centre stage in their community-type work. Whether volunteer victim support workers wish to become involved in such activities when there are many victims needing help is another issue. As has already been argued, victim support can play an important, if not vital part, through their work with victims but targetting victims to 'deliver' crime prevention activities becomes problematic for example, where perpetrators and victims are known to each other.

Thirdly, it was found that community development, in terms of promoting social integration, did not necessarily reduce crime and the fear of crime. The victimisation survey results and victim interviews both suggested that pockets of social cohesion, i.e., friendly neighbouring did not include sufficient control mechanisms to demonstrate that crime and anti-social activity were prevented. Nor were friendly neighbours less afraid of being victimised in the future. This is in line with other findings (DuBow and Emmons, 1981; Greenberg et al 1985; Rosenbaum, 1988; Demuth, 1989). There were, however, some types of action that could have had positive results. It seemed important to turn around the negative social climate on the estate. This might be achieved through supporting some community leaders (Power, 1989) and developing community organisations. Not all types of community organisations have the capacity to reduce crime (Skogan, 1988) but the level of organisation seems to have an impact on crime (Kohfield et al, 1981). The findings of this study point towards the importance of mediating conflicts as part of a strategy to create a more positive and 'healthy' environment within which residents may be able to take more effective preventive actions themselves. Inter-personal conflicts contributed to residents' feelings of lack of safety. The lack of fit between residents' concerns and agencies' preoccupations suggests that statutory and voluntary agencies should be more responsive to the problems of residents and this should be an integral part of a development strategy (also see Shaftoe, 1986).

Finally, broader issues were raised about crime prevention advice. For many incidents of personal crimes, particularly when the assailant and victim knew each other, which was generally the case, giving advice was not always an appropriate response to the situation. For other incidents it was difficult to give advice that did not unnecessarily curtail the life-styles of victims (most victims of personal incidents were under the age of 30). In the interviews, victims spontaneously gave accounts of how they protect themselves in their everyday life. Indeed, one of the residents' main concerns were for their personal safety and the safety of their families. It emerged from these accounts that both men and women took protective actions, and were in a state of alert, both in their homes and on the streets (see also Stanko, 1990). But some victims seemed better at protecting themselves than others. One victim clearly made the point.

My boyfriend's father was burgled and I could not understand why he hadn't organised his things in a more protective way... If I go away for weekends I always have to do an eccentric hiding of things.. [and] when I was on my own I had a light show. I wired this synchronized programme of lights and the radio (Victim in her 20s).

Information given to workers on crime prevention advice might build on the more effective actions people have already adopted (women seemed to take different and more elaborate precautions than men). Not all the types of protective actions would be suitable, for example, having large dogs in small flats (one woman said 'I feel safe here because I have a rottweiler who attacks strangers') or iron doors that on occasions are difficult to open quickly even by emergency services. More subtle and appropriate strategies were described by other victims; carrying small amounts of change in several different pockets (a male victim), or keeping hands out of their coat pockets (young woman victim). Another woman victim adopted a different approach:

There are a lot of people wandering around but generally you can place them. You've got a pretty good idea which stranger belongs where. I make an effort to say "Hi" to everyone I see just to get an acknowledgement from them, so that they know that I know they're there (Victim in her 20s).

More elaborate ideas involved making sure friends waited until residents were safely in their flats before they left them, or collecting family members from train stations to walk back across the estate. A victim said how worried her family were about her living on the estate, especially after she'd been attacked, and they had the following safety arrangement:

I talk with my daughter everyday on the phone. I tell her if I'm going out. She wants to know where I am. If I don't answer the phone at 10ish she is in her car and down here straight away (Victim in her 60s).

The use of the telephone was a recurring theme when victims talked about protecting themselves. Regular calls to see if family members had 'got back home safely', the swapping of numbers between friends, and ringing friends up if they were frightened, were all strategies pursued by victims. Those who had no telephones talked of moments of extreme anxiety because they were unable to call 'any of the emergency services'.

Building on the many safety precautions undertaken by residents, and encouraging the extention of existing preventive activities offers, at least in the short term, the hope of respite from crime.

APPENDIX

Interviews with Victims

The details of those who were interviewed were as follows;
— 18 were women and 9 were men
— 23 were white and 4 were black (two men and two women)
— 10 were aged between 16 and 30 years
— 9 aged between 31 and 59 years
— 8 were aged 60 and over

The sample was chosen by taking 40 victims referred consecutively to the police during the first year and 12 victims referred consecutively during the second year. The first name for the sample was taken six months prior to the letter sent out to ask the victim if they would meet the researcher.

In the first year:
— 2 children were excluded from the final analysis for this paper
— 4 victims had moved
— 2 victims refused to be interviewed
— 1 victim had a contagious illness
— 6 victims were not found in after 3 or more calls
— 4 victims were not in after 1 or 2 calls
A total of 21 victims were interviewed.

In the second year:
— 1 victim was not willing to be interviewed
— 5 victims were not in after 3 or more calls
A total of 6 victims were interviewed.

References

Blagg, H., G. Pearson, A. Sampson, D. Smith, P. Stubbs (1988). 'Inter-agency co-ordination: rhetoric and reality' in eds. T. Hope and M. Shaw *Communities and Crime Reduction.* London: HMSO.

Bottoms, A. E., and P. Wiles (1986). 'Housing Tenure and Residential Community Crime Careers in Britain' in eds. A. J. Reiss and M. Tonry *Communities and Crime.* Crime and Justice: A Review of Research. Volume 8. Chicago: University of Chicago.

Bulmer, M. (1986). *Neighbours: The Work of Philip Abrams.* London: Cambridge University Press.

Demuth, C. (1989). *Community Safety in Brighton.* Brighton Council Police and Public Safety Unit.

Dubow, F., and D. Emmons (1981). 'The Community Hypothesis' in ed. D. A. Lewis *Reactions to Crime.* Beverley Hills: Sage Publications.

Forrester, D., M. Chatterton, K. Pease and R. Brown (1988). *The Kirkholt Burglary Prevention Project, Rochdale.* Crime Prevention Unit Paper 13. Home Office: Crime Prevention Unit.

Forrester, D., S. Frenz, M. O'connell, K. Pease (1990). *The Kirkholt Burglary Prevention Project: Phase II.* Crime Prevention Unit Paper 23. Home Office: Crime Prevention Unit.

Genn, H. (1988). 'Multiple Victimisation' in eds. M. Maguire and J. Pointing *Victims of Crime: A New Deal?* Milton Keynes: Open University Press.

Geraghty, J. (1990). *Crime Prevention: An Impact on Probation Practice.* Crime Prevention Unit Paper 24. Home Office: Crime Prevention Unit.

Greenberg, S. W., W. M. Rohe, and J. R. Williams (1985). *Informal Citizen Action and Crime Prevention at the Neighbourhood Level.* U.S. Department of Justice: National Institute of Justice.

Home Office (1989). *Criminal Statistics, England and Wales.* London: Home Office.

Hope, T. (1985). *Implementing Crime Prevention Measures.* Home Office Research Study 86. London: HMSO.

Hope, T., and M. Shaw (1988). eds *Communities and Crime Reduction.* London: HMSO.

Knight, B., and R. Hayes (1981). *Self Help in the Inner City.* London: Voluntary Services Council.

Kohfield, C. W., B. Salert, and S. Schoenberg (1981). 'Neighbourhood Associations and Urban Crime' in *Community Action* Nov/Dec.

Lavrakas, P. J., and S. F. Bennett (1989). *A Process and Impact Evaluation of the 1983-86 Neighbourhood Anti-Crime Self-Help Program: Summary Report*. Illinois: Centre for Urban Affairs and Policy Research.

Laycock, G. (1989). *An evaluation of Domestic Security Surveys*. Crime Prevention Unit Paper 18. London: Home Office.

Maguire, M., and C. Corbett (1987). *The effects of Crime and the Work of Victims Support Schemes*. London: Gower.

Marshall, T. (1990). *Crime and Accountability*. London: HMSO.

Newburn, T., and S. Merry (1990). *Keeping in Touch: Police-Victim Communication in Two Areas*. Home Office Research Study 116. London: HMSO.

Newman, O. (1981). *Community of Interest*. Garden City: Anchor.

Podolefsky, A., and F. Dubow (1981). *Strategies for Community Crime Prevention*. (Illinois: Charles C. Thomas).

Power, A. (1989). 'Housing, Community and Crime' in ed. D. Downes *Crime and the City*. London: Macmillan.

Reynolds, F. (1986). *The Problem Housing Estate: An Account of Omega and its People*. Aldershot: Gower.

Rosenbaum, D. P. (1987). 'The Theory and Research Behind Neighbourhood Watch: Is It a Sound Strategy?' *Crime and Delinquency*, Vol 33 No.1. pp103–134.

Rosenbaum, D. P. (1988). 'Community Crime Prevention: A Review and Synthesis of the Literature' *Justice Quarterly*, Vol 5, No.3. pp323–395.

Safe Neighbourhoods Unit (1985). *After Entryphones: Improving Management and Security in Multi-Storey Blocks*. London: Safe Neighbourhoods Unit.

Safe Neighbourhoods Unit (undated). *Report of the Unit's Work 1981-1986* London: Safe Neighbourhood Unit.

Sampson, A., P. Stubbs, D. Smith, G. Pearson, H. Blagg (1988). 'Crime, localities and the multi-agency approach', *British Journal of Criminology*, 28, pp478–493.

Sampson, A., and G. Farrell (1990). *Victim Support and Crime Prevention in an Inner-City Setting*. Crime Prevention Unit Paper 21. London: Home Office.

Sampson, A., and D. Smith (1990). 'Probation and Community Crime Prevention', unpublished paper given at National Association of Probation Officers Conference, Otterburn, May.

Shaftoe, H. (1986). *Crime Prevention the Case for a Neighbourhood-based Approach*. Edinburgh: SACRO.

Shapland, J., J. Willmore, P. Duff (1985). *Victims in the Criminal Justice System*. Aldershot: Gower.

Shapland, J., and J. Vagg (1988). *Policing by the Public*. London: Routledge.

Sheppard, J. (1988). 'Supporting Victims of Violent Crime' *British Medical Journal*. Vol.297. 26 November.

Skogan, W. G. (1988). 'Community Organisations and Crime' in ed. A. Reiss and M. Tonry *Crime and Justice*. Annual Review of Research. Chicago: University of Chicago Press.

Stanko, E. (1990). *Everyday Violence*. London: Pandora.

Williams, Karen (1983). *Community Resources for Victims of Crime*. Research and Planning Unit Paper No.14. London: Home Office.

Wilson, R. (1963). *Difficult Housing Estates*. Tavistock Pamphlet no.5. London: Tavistock Publications.

Crime Prevention Unit Papers

1. **Reducing Burglary: a study of chemists' shops.**
   Gloria Laycock. 1985. v + 7pp. (0 86353 154 8).
2. **Reducing Crime: developing the role of crime prevention panels.**
   Lorna J.F. Smith and Gloria Laycock. 1985. v + 14pp. (0 86252 189 0).
3. **Property Marking: a deterrant to domestic burglary?**
   Gloria Laycock. 1985. v + 25pp. (0 86252 193 9).
4. **Designing for Car Security: towards a crime free car.**
   Dean Southall and Paul Ekblom. 1985. v + 25pp. (0 86252 222 6).
5. **The Prevention of Shop Theft: an approach through crime analysis.**
   Paul Ekblom. 1986 v + 19pp. (0 86252 237 4).
6. **Prepayment Coin Meters: a target for burglary.**
   Nigel Hill. 1986. v + 15pp. (086252 245 5).
7. **Crime in Hospitals: diagnosis and prevention.**
   Lorna J.F. Smith 1987. v + 25pp. (086252 267 6).
8. **Preventing Juvenile Crime: the Staffordshire Experience.**
   Kevin Heal and Gloria Laycock. 1987. v + 29pp. (086252 297 8).
9. **Preventing Robberies at Sub-Post Offices: an evaluation of a security initiative.** Paul Ekblom. 1987. v + 34pp. (086252 300 1).
10. **Getting the Best Out of Crime Analysis.**
    Paul Ekblom. 1988. v + 38pp. (0 86252 307 8).
11. **Retail Crime: Prevention through Crime Analysis.**
    John Burrows. 1988. v + 30pp. (0 86252 313 3).
12. **Neighbourhood Watch in England and Wales: a locational analysis.**
    Sohail Husain. 1988. v + 63pp. (0 86252 314 1).
13. **The Kirkholt Burglary Prevention Project, Rochdale.** David Forrester, Mike Chatterton and Ken Pease with the assistance of Robin Brown. 1988. v + 34pp. (0 86252 333 8).
14. **The Prevention of Robbery at Building Society Branches.** Claire Austin. 1988. v + 18pp. (0 86252 337 0).
15. **Crime and Racial Harrassment in Asian-run Small Shops: the scope for prevention.** Paul Ekblom and Frances Simon with the assistance of Sneh Birdi. 1988. v + 54pp. (0 86252 348 6).
16. **Crime and Nuisance in the Shopping Centre: a case study in crime prevention.** Susan Phillips and Raymond Cochrane. 1988. v + 32pp. (0 86252 358 3).
17. **The Prevention of Fraud.** Michael Levi. 1988. v + 19pp. (0 86252 359/1).
18. **An Evaluation of Domestic Security Surveys.** Gloria Laycock. 1989. v + 33pp. (0 86252 408 3).
19. **Downtown Drinkers: the perceptions and fears of the public in a city centre.** Malcolm Ramsay. 1989. v + 23pp. (0 86252 419 9).
20. **The Management and Prevention of Juvenile Crime Problems.**
    Barrymore Cooper. 1989. v + 63pp. (0 86252 420 2).
21. **Victim Support and Crime Prevention in an Inner-City Setting.** Alice Sampson and Graham Farrell. 1990. v + 27pp. (0 86252 504 7).
22. **Lagerland Lost? An Experiment in Keeping Drinkers off the Street in Central Coventry and Elsewhere.** Malcolm Ramsay. 1990. v + 38pp. (0 86252 520 9).

23. **The Kirtholt Burglary Prevention Project: Phase II.** David Forrester, Samantha Frenz, Martin O'Connell and Ken Pease. 1990. v + 51pp. (0 862562)

24. **Probation Practice in Crime Prevention.** Jane Geraghty. 1991. v + 45pp. (0 86252 605 1)